DATE DUE

OCT 10			
FEB 3			
MAY 19			
NOV 16			
JUN 1			
OCT 25 2005			
DEC 08 2005			
FEB 02 2006			
FEB 09 2006			

FOLLETT

Animal World

Eagles

Christine Butterworth and Donna Bailey

STECK-VAUGHN
LIBRARY
A Division of Steck-Vaughn Company

Can you see the eagle high in the sky?
It is a golden eagle.
Golden eagles have brown feathers
on their bodies.
The feathers on their heads and at the back
of their necks are a golden color.

2

Golden eagles like to nest up high.
This nest is on a high rocky ledge
in the mountains.
The eagles use the same nest every year.

An eagle's nest is called an aerie.
Some aeries are very big and old.
Eagles use the same aerie
for many years.
This aerie is about ten feet wide!

4

The eagles return to their nest
in the winter.
They bring large sticks to mend it.
They line the nest with grass and leaves.

The female eagle is bigger than the male.
They fly together before they mate.
The male shows the female
how well he can fly.
He dives down very fast and then swoops
up again.

In the spring, the female eagle lays
two eggs in the nest.
She sits on them to keep them warm.
The eggs hatch after seven weeks.

The female eagle hears the baby eaglets
making a noise inside the eggs.
Then the eaglets break the eggs open
with their beaks.

The eaglets have fluffy white down
on their bodies.
Their feathers will grow later.
They stay by their mother to keep warm.

The male eagle hunts for food
to bring back to the nest.
The female tears off bits of meat
to give to the eaglets.

The eaglets are four weeks old now.
Can you see the dark tips on their wings?
These are the new feathers growing.

Now the female flies off to find food.

The eaglets are alone in the nest.

They keep very still.

It is not safe when their mother is away.

12

The male eagle keeps watch.
A wildcat comes to look for
some baby birds to eat.
The male eagle flies down and
chases the wildcat away.

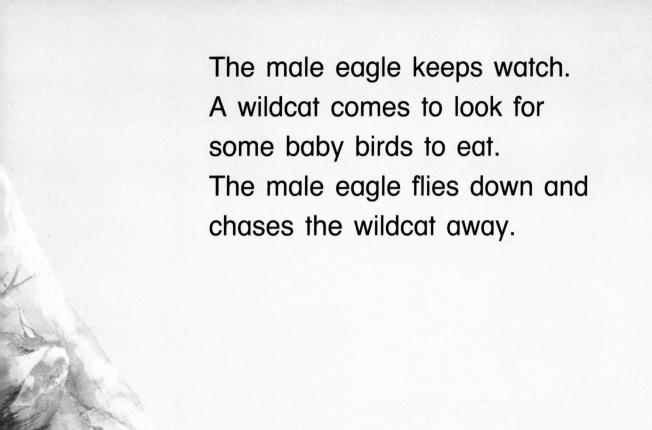

It is late summer.

The eaglets have grown all their feathers.

They are getting ready to fly.

One of them takes off from the nest.
It wobbles a bit, but it soon learns
to fly.
The other eaglet will soon follow it.

15

The eaglets must learn to hunt
before the winter comes.
Then it will be time for them to leave
the nest and live on their own.

Now it is winter.
This eagle is fully grown.
She looks for her food in the snow.
Soon she will find a mate and they will
look for an aerie in the mountains where
she can lay her eggs.

A golden eagle has broad wings that
help it float on the wind.
When an eagle spreads out its wings,
they are almost seven feet across.

This eagle is hunting for food.
It flies high into the sky.
It has sharp eyes that can see a rabbit
almost a mile away.

When a rabbit comes out of its hole,
the eagle sees it.
The eagle swoops down to the ground.
It catches the rabbit with its feet.

The eagle has sharp claws on its feet.
They dig in and hold the rabbit.
Then the eagle kills the rabbit with
its hooked beak.

Golden eagles eat foxes and other animals,
as well as rabbits.
If its prey is too heavy to carry,
the eagle pulls the animal apart with
its claws and beak.

This sea eagle catches fish.
It eats ducks and birds, too.
Sometimes it steals fish
from smaller birds.

The sea eagle flies over the water.
When it sees a fish just under the surface,
the eagle catches the fish in its claws and
pulls it out of the water.

The sea eagle makes its nest
on a high cliff.
It can be safe there.
Nobody can climb up
to steal its eggs.

These bald eagles live in North America.
Bald eagles are not really bald.
They have white feathers on their heads.
The feathers on their bodies
are brown, and their tails are white.

This bald eagle is eating
a dead sea lion which has been
washed up on the beach.
Lots of bald eagles come to feed on it.

This eagle has eaten so much meat that
its stomach is full.
Now it will not need to eat for two days.

When the weather gets colder,
the bald eagles fly south to
a warmer part of the country.
They will spend the winter there.

There are not many bald eagles left.
Some of them have been shot
by hunters and farmers.
Some people catch them and use them
to hunt other animals for sport.

Many eagles have died because of
poison in the fish and animals
that they eat.
The poison comes from sprays that
farmers use on their crops.

People are now trying to protect eagles,
so the eagles will not die out.
There are laws to stop thieves from
stealing eggs from their nests and
laws to stop hunters from shooting them.

Index

Reading Consultant: Diana Bentley
Editorial Consultant: Donna Bailey
Supervising Editor: Kathleen Fitzgibbon

Illustrated by Paula Chasty
Picture research by Suzanne Williams
Designed by Richard Garratt Design

Photographs
Cover: Frank Lane Picture Agency/Leonard Lee Rue
Bruce Coleman: title page (Erwin & Peggy Bauer), 7, 8, 9 and 14 (Dennis
    Green), 10 and 11 (J. L. G. Grande), 15 (G. Ziesler), 16 (W. W. F./Eric
    Dracesco), 17 (Hans Reinhard), 21 (Jeff Foott), 22 (Leonard Lee Rue),
    23 and 24 (Dieter & Mary Plage), 26 (Charlie Ott), 27 (Bob and Clara
    Calhoun), 28 (Steven C. Kaufman)
Frank Lane Picture Agency: 2 (M. Newman), 3 (D. Dugan), 6 (Philip Perry)
Eric & David Hosking: 25 and 32
ZEFA: 20 and 29

Library of Congress Cataloging-in-Publication Data: Butterworth, Christine. Eagles / Christine Butterworth and Donna
[illustrated by Paula Chasty]. p. cm. — (Animal world) SUMMARY: Describes the characteristics and habits of eagles. I
0-8114-2632-7 1. Eagles—Juvenile literature. [1. Eagles.] I. Bailey, Donna. II. Chasty, Paula, ill. III. Title. IV. Series: A
world (Austin, Tex.) QL696.F32B88 1990 598′.916—dc20 89-26076 CIP AC